Smelly Old History

WARTIME WHIFFS

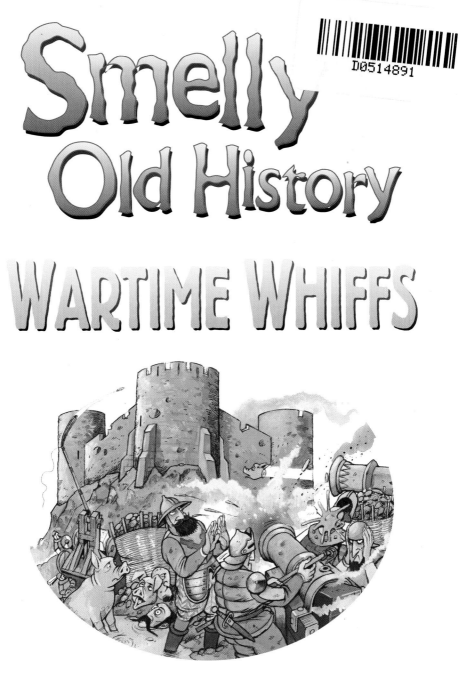

Mary Dobson

OXFORD UNIVERSITY PRESS

Oxford University Press, Great Clarendon Street, Oxford OX2 6DP

Oxford New York
Athens Auckland Bangkok Bogotá Buenos Aires Calcutta
Cape Town Chennai Dar es Salaam Delhi Florence Hong Kong Istanbul
Karachi Kuala Lumpur Madrid Melbourne Mexico City Mumbai
Nairobi Paris São Paulo Singapore Taipei Tokyo Toronto Warsaw
and associated companies in Berlin Ibadan

Oxford is a registered trade mark of Oxford University Press

Published in the United States
by Oxford University Press Inc., New York

© Mary Dobson 1998
The moral rights of the author have been asserted
First published 1998

Artwork: Vince Reid. Photographs reproduced by kind permission of:
Imperial War Museum: p11, p17; Imperial War Museum / Bruce Bainsfather p26

British Library Cataloguing in Publication Data available

ISBN 0 19 910530 8

1 3 5 7 9 10 8 6 4 2

Printed in Great Britain

CONTENTS

A SENSE OF THE PAST 4

STINKING SOLDIERS 6

BREATHTAKING BEASTS 8

WHIFFY WEAPONS 10

STINKERS AND INCAS 12

NAVAL NASTIES 14

ROTTEN RATIONS 16

BOOTS AND BUGS 18

OVERPOWERING PERFUMES 20

A MESSY MISTAKE 22

MOPPING UP THE MESS 24

THE STENCH OF THE TRENCH 26

CHILDREN SCRATCH AND SNIFF 28

PUNGENT PUZZLES & GLOSSARY 30

TIMELINE 31

INDEX 32

Scratch the scented panels lightly with a
fingernail to release their smell.

A Sense of the Past

Take a deep breath and prepare for battle. Feel the weight of a splendid suit of armour on your sweaty body. Touch (gently!) your glistening sword. Add an extra bit of spit to shine your boots. Listen to the deafening roar of cannons filling the air. Taste the scent of victory. There's plenty of wartime excitement to stimulate your senses. But be prepared for a whole new sensation — wars could be horribly smelly!

History books usually leave out the smelly bits. This book gives you a whiff of the real thing — there's more in here than meets the eye. Scratch and sniff the pungent panels to recall the wartime whiffs of the past.

Just getting his armour on is a sweaty ordeal for this soldier.

This Native American, Bad Hand, is really dressed to kill.

Since ancient times, men and women (and children) have fought bloody battles. Wars have been waged over land, sea and air. Many have died for king and country. We remember the heroic actions of famous generals and unknown soldiers. We gasp at the terrible tragedies of death and destruction. Some wars seem terribly pointless. Others have changed the course of history. Most have been mucky and messy. Read on to sniff out the smelly side....

Youngsters got bogged down in the muck in the Children's Crusade to the Holy Land in 1212.

This African warrior is ready for action.

Molly Pitcher jumped into action when her husband was killed in the American War of Independence.

STINKING SOLDIERS

The war cry goes up: your country needs you! Across the centuries and all over the world, soldiers and civilians have rushed into battle. Some soldiers have been trained since childhood for the big event. They can't wait! Poor peasants have sometimes welcomed a breath of battle air to spice up their odorous life. Others have been press-ganged into action. Take a look at these soldiers as they prepare for the offensive.

This 3rd-century (AD) Roman soldier has been patiently guarding the border between Scotland and Roman Britain — he'll be relieved when there's a wee bit of action.

This 15th-century Japanese samurai warrior is an expert in martial arts. He carries two swords — a long one for fighting and a short one to hack off the heads of dead enemies, or cut through his own belly, rather than face the shame of defeat. Before the battle, he takes a bath — at least he knows he'll die clean and pure.

French and English soldiers at the Battle of Agincourt in 1415 had to be prepared for action — especially when they were attacked from behind. This poor archer has swapped a life of muck and manure back home for a gory glory — but like many of his mates, he isn't prepared for an attack of dysentery and diarrhoea.

Drinking time's up for this stinky sailor. In the Napoleonic Wars (1793-1815) press-gang officers sneaked into taverns to force unsuspecting folk to join up. At least this chap's used to bloody brawls.

BREATHTAKING BEASTS

Many armies in the past have included breathtaking beasts in their ranks. Horses, camels and even elephants have marched into battle, straining under the weight of their riders.

A famous general called Hannibal led his herd of elephants across the frozen Alps into Italy. He'd heard news of a massive Roman takeover and decided two could play at that game. In 218 BC, he slithered up and down the Alps with his great team of African war-elephants, 10,000 horses and 50,000 foot soldiers. By the time Hannibal reached Italy he only had 37 elephants left. But it was enough to put the wind up the Romans.

Hannibal's elephants had specially sharpened tusks to gore the enemy. The Roman horses were disgusted by the elephants' smell and reeled over. After some vile victories, Hannibal was finally defeated by the Romans at the Battle of Zama in 202 BC.

Scratch and sniff this honking horror.

Three thousand years ago the ancient Greeks came up with a real stinker — they packed their men off to fight the Trojans cooped up in a wooden horse.

The Trojans thought it was a nice little present from the gods and wheeled it into their walled city. But inside this breathtaking beast were a whole lot of gruesome Greeks! In the dead of night, the Greeks dropped out of its smelly belly and opened the gates of the city. In stormed an entire army to destroy Troy.

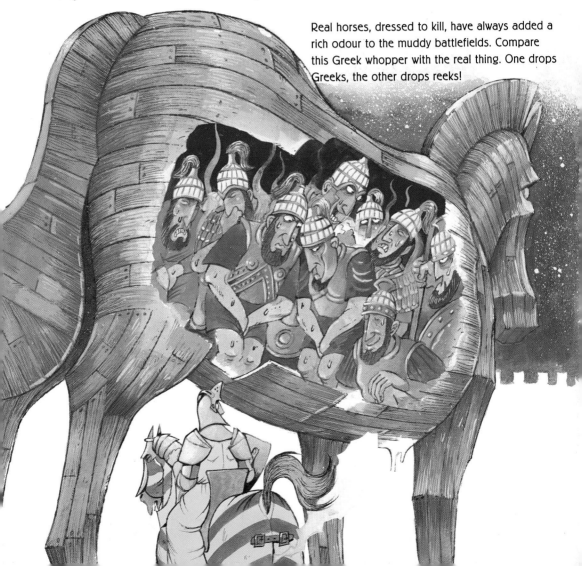

Real horses, dressed to kill, have always added a rich odour to the muddy battlefields. Compare this Greek whopper with the real thing. One drops Greeks, the other drops reeks!

WHIFFY WEAPONS

Some of the world's worst inventions have been deadly weapons.

Slurping spear

Shaka, the 19th-century South African Zulu warrior, had a special stabbing spear. He named it 'klwa' after the slurping noise it made when drawn out of its victim's flesh.

Grisly guns

Gunpowder was first used by the Chinese in the 7th century. But guess where it really comes from — rotting pigs' manure! Once the Europeans got a whiff of its smelly effects, they were hot on the scent.

In this scene, medieval crusaders are firing cannons, guns and trebuchets (catapults) at their Turkish enemies — they've popped in some rotting pigs' heads too!

Fatal fire

'Greek fire' must be one of the foulest ancient wartime whiffs. It was a mysterious liquid that burst into flames when it was thrown on to water, and it couldn't be extinguished by pure water.

There's only one solution. These 12th-century Saracen warriors are taking aim with buckets of urine. The potash in the urine soon quenches the stench.

Gas masks in the First World War.

Ghastly gases

In the First World War (1914-18), chlorine gas was known as 'the devil's breath'. Soldiers soaked their shirts in urine and held them to their noses to protect themselves from the deadly fumes. Mustard gas was especially dangerous as it had no smell.

Stinky bombs

The Chinese fired stink bombs in the 14th century — made from a mixture of human excrement and gunpowder. Their effect was unbelievably foul.

When war took to the skies in the 20th century, exploding bombs wiped out huge areas. In the Second World War (1939-45), Doodlebugs or 'Buzz Bombs' flew without pilots and caused massive damage. The first atomic bomb was dropped on Hiroshima in Japan in 1945. Its effect was so devastating that it quickly brought an end to the Second World War.

A doodlebug

STINKERS AND INCAS

Many armies have been defeated by deadly weapons. Others have been defeated by deadly diseases. Smallpox and measles spread like wildfire through the Americas in the 16th century, wiping out the Inca and Aztec civilizations and killing more people than any whiffy weapons.

Follow the story of Pizarro and Atahualpa, to see how an entire civilization of several million Incas was crushed by a small band of stinking soldiers and sailors.

The Incas were an amazing civilization in South America — Atahualpa, their king, was worshipped like a god.

In 1532, the Incas are in for a shock. A small band of 180 Spanish conquistadores (conquerors), led by Pizarro, roll up out of the blue and take a fancy to the rich, golden objects of the Incas. The Incas do their best to welcome their stinking visitors. They wonder what their strange animals and weapons are for.

Before long, the Incas find out — Pizarro and his men fire at the Incas. Atahualpa is taken prisoner and put to death.

But the worst warfare whiff is yet to come. The conquistadores are loaded with deadly germs such as smallpox and measles. One sniff of their poisonous breath is enough to snuff out the Incas.

NAVAL NASTIES

Many battles have been fought on the oceans. Take to the high seas in 1805 with Admiral Lord Nelson on HMS *Victory* at the Battle of Trafalgar. Nelson is sailing straight into the line of the French and Spanish. Above the roar of cannonballs, he issues his famous last words: 'England expects that every man will do his duty.' See just what he expects...

His mate has not done his duty — he's refused to mop up the officers' mess. His punishment is severe — he's being flogged to death with a cat-o'nine-tails.

Balanced by the pissdale, this sailor has to brave the elements — it's not much fun when the wind's blowing in the wrong direction.

Risking his life, Lord Nelson stands proudly on the quarter-deck . . . but not for long. He's already lost an eye and an arm. At the Battle of Trafalgar, he wins a victory but loses his life.

Firing cannonballs is a non-stop business — this chap dutifully waits to be relieved.

Deep in the belly of the ship, the ship's surgeon keeps busy hacking off injured bits. The stench is overpowering, but at least the floor is painted red to disguise the sight of blood.

ROTTEN RATIONS

Living and sleeping conditions for the military in the past were usually appalling. So too were their revolting rations of food. Sample a few of these rotten reminders.

Roman reeks
Roman rations consisted of garlic, onions, cheese, vinegary wine — and more garlic. It's not surprising that Roman soldiers reeked.

Fresh supplies
Mongol warriors in the 13th century were trained not to complain — they survived for long periods on curdled mare's milk and meat from their horses. When desperate, they drank blood from their horse's neck.

Marching maggots
Soldiers in the English Civil War (1642-49) were given their daily rations of 'marching food' — a handful of hard biscuits and a lump of mouldy meat or cheese. No-one liked to mention the maggots which came with these tasty treats.

Scratch and sniff for a foul cheesy whiff.

Limeys

Food on board ship had to last for months, but most of it went rotten fairly quickly. Imagine a diet of putrid porridge, salted and slimy meat, fish soup with boiled worms and maggots, cheese so hard you can use it to make buttons — all washed down with a daily dose of eight pints of beer. Many suffered terribly from their foul diet — their gums rotted and their legs went black. In the late 18th century, the British Navy tried to stop the rot — they squeezed limes and lemons into the rations which prevented scurvy.

We want your KITCHEN WASTE

PIG FOOD

KEEP IT DRY, FREE FROM GLASS, BONES, METAL, PAPER, ETC. IT ALSO FEEDS POULTRY. YOUR COUNCIL WILL COLLECT

Bacon rations

In the Second World War, food rations were in short supply, and everyone was encouraged to keep pigs! The swimming bath of the ladies' Carlton Club in Pall Mall in London was converted into a giant pigsty.

BOOTS AND BUGS

Cheesy rations were bad enough, but cheesy boots caked in mud took some beating! Over the centuries, millions of pairs of boots have been made for marching troops. Just imagine the poor feet inside them — blistered, bleeding and often blue with cold.

Clothing was another stinky issue. The medieval crusaders took along washerwomen to do their dirty work, but throughout history most soldiers had to live, sleep and fight in filthy uniforms. They were often infested with bugs and lice which spread horrible diseases, such as typhus.

Take a look at these Union soldiers in the American Civil War (1861-65) as they set up camp. This war was fought between Confederates (from the southern states) and Union forces (from the northern states), but the bugs don't care whose side they're on. Shortage of boots became a serious problem for the Confederates. Many of them had to be excluded from the battlefield because they didn't have decent footwear.

OVERPOWERING PERFUMES

Some armies used loads of perfumes and powders to freshen up their soldiers and mask the rotten battle odours.

Powder puffs

Soldiers in the American Revolution, or War of Independence (1775-83), lavishly greased their hair with fat then added flour. They made so much mess, they had to be given special powder rooms.

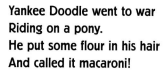

Yankee Doodle went to war
Riding on a pony.
He put some flour in his hair
And called it macaroni!

Napoleon's 'eau'ders

The French general Napoleon made sure he had all his favourite perfumes on his campaigns (1799-1815). Every so often, he would nip into his tent and slosh on a bit of eau-de-cologne.

Overpowering perfumes weren't to everyone's liking. In the English Civil War (1642-49) and the French Revolution (1789-91), people in the same country were fighting against each other on different sides: the scented and unscented sides!

Smell the difference!

In the uncivil English war, you could usually smell the difference between an English cavalier or royalist (who supported King Charles I) and a roundhead or parliamentarian (who supported Oliver Cromwell). King Charles and his cavaliers loved perfumes, Cromwell and his puritan followers preferred the smell of pure body odour.

Scratch and sniff to see which is the royalist.

Revolting revolutionaries

In the late 18th century, French peasants were revolted by the wealth of the aromatic aristocracy. The French king, Louis XVI, and his queen, Marie Antoinette, reeked of perfume. When the peasants stormed the Bastille prison in 1789, they deliberately soiled their rags with foul stinks — just to show how revolting they were.

In both the English Civil War and the French Revolution, it was a victory for the unscented side, and the fragrant monarchs lost their heads.

A MESSY MISTAKE

Planning and carrying out a military campaign needed skill and correct information. One false move and it was into the valley of death. The most spectacular military blunder was the Charge of the Light Brigade in the Crimean War (1854-56), in Russia. Try following this messy mix-up.

The French, Brits and Turks are fighting against the Russians. The British Lord Cardigan pulls over his Light Brigade and surveys the scene.

Up rushes young Captain Nolan with an urgent order from Lord Raglan, Commander of the British Army.

The Chief orders you to stop the Russians taking our guns.

Which guns?

Spot the difference.

Into the Valley of Death rode the six hundred.

Lord Cardigan survived and soaked up his blood, sweat and tears in a bath with a bottle of champagne — to his relief, he was not fired by the British Army after this appallingly messy mistake.

MOPPING UP THE MESS

Dealing with the dead and wounded has always been a grisly affair.

Terrible trophies

The ancient Celts hung their enemies' heads on their horses as war trophies. The smell must have been atrocious.

The Aztecs proudly roasted prisoners of war over hot fires of chilli pepper — they believed their sun-god needed a daily top-up of human blood and hearts.

Missing bits

After the Battle of Waterloo in 1815, dentists did a roaring trade — teeth from the slain were made into dentures, known as 'Waterloos'.

One English officer serving under the Duke of Wellington in the Peninsular War (1808-14) is reported to have had his arm removed without even wincing, and then to have called out:'Here, bring that arm back! There's a ring my wife gave me on the finger.'

The hooves of Napoleon's favourite horse, Marengo, were whipped off when the horse died in 1812 and made into snuff boxes — these were filled with spicy tobacco and passed round at dinner parties. Imagine enjoying a horsy whiff with each smelly sniff.

Stopping the rot

The wounded have been treated by doctors and nurses with all sorts of smelly solutions — perfumes, alcohol, herbs, marshmallow, burning tar, and hot irons. Some have made great attempts to stop the rot.

The Romans built hospitals called Valetudinaria on the battlefield, to mop up the wounded as quickly as possible.

In the 16th century, a French army surgeon, Ambroise Paré, was horrified to see the agonising results of scorching gunshot wounds with burning oil. He tried yolks of eggs, oil of roses, and turpentine, bringing fragrant relief to many soldiers.

During the Crimean War (1854-56), Florence Nightingale and Mary Seacole made sparkling changes by cleaning up the horrible stenches at the army hospital at Scutari.

When Florence Nightingale arrived at the hospital she found that the floors were covered with the contents of the latrines. The wounded men had to paddle through this every time they answered the call of nature.

This scene shows the hospital before and after she worked her magic.

THE STENCH OF THE TRENCH

During the First World War (1914-18) thousands of soldiers on both sides ended up in the trenches across northern Europe. The stench was horrific. Squelching in slime and mud, nibbled by rats and lice, unwashed and underfed, soldiers did their best to brave their odorous ordeals.

One man cheered up his mates with a letter from his mum:
'My mum says to send home my socks for washing.'
Another said: 'I adore war — nobody grumbles at you for being dirty. It's great fun not having to wash, or take off my boots.'

Cartoonists offered some light relief.

" Well, if you knows of a better 'ole, go to it "

But the reality was far from amusing, and for many who survived the whiff of war lingered long after peace was declared at 11 am. on 11 November 1918.

The Smell of War
I still remember all too well
That evil, rotting, hateful smell.
The smell of rats, the smell of death,
The foul and rancid soldiers' breath.
The pits we dug within our trench
To bury all our human stench.
The poison gas that lingers still,
The greasy guns we used to kill.
I shut my eyes, try not to think
Of all that mud and filth and stink.
I'm haunted now I'm old and grey,
That smell of war won't go away.

CHILDREN SCRATCH & SNIFF

Wars have torn people apart, but they've also brought people together. Children throughout history have learnt to cope with new situations, new friends, and new smells!

When the Second World War broke out in 1939, thousands of children in London were packed off to the countryside to protect them from the bombs dropped by German planes.

Tom and Gertrude are evacuees sent to a new home in the countryside. Toffee-nosed Tom takes an instant dislike to the stench of farm manure and pigs! Grubby little Gertrude loves the fresh air of the countryside. But she's not very happy when Mrs Trotter tells her to change her vest — it's stuffed with newspapers and a lump of goose fat. Her mother just gives her an annual spring-clean to remove the lice.

Scratch and sniff for a farmyard whiff.

Within a month Tom and Gerry are best friends...

While they're away, no bombs fall so the children return to London. This was known as The Phoney War. But on 7 September 1940, the real Blitz begins. Tom and Gerry find themselves huddled together in an Anderson Shelter in the black-out. Their gas masks are full of sweat, snot and saliva, and their hair is itchy, but at least they can't sniff the foul fumes of the burning bombs outside.

For children like Tom and Gerry, the war was a tough time. Years later, when their grandchildren turn up their noses at school dinners or scratch their lousy little heads, they remember the wartime whiffs they had to put up with.

PUNGENT PUZZLES

Cracking codes

Armies sent secret messages in code language. The Roman General, Julius Caesar, moved letters three places, so that A became D, B became E, etc. When he conquered Britain, his Latin message read:

> YHQL, YLGL, YLFL = VENI, VIDI, VICI:
> this means 'I came, I saw, I conquered.

Using the same system, work out these smelly messages:

L   VPHOO   D   UDW

L   VPHOO   BRXU   ERRWV

ZKHUH   KDYH   BRX   KLGGHQ   WKH   PRXOGB   UDWLRQV?

— LQ   WKH   VWLQNLQJ   UXEELVK!

GLOSSARY

atomic bomb	a bomb which uses atomic energy and causes massive destruction
brigade	a group of troops
civil war	a war between peoples of one country
doodlebug	a flying bomb used in the Second World War
dysentery	a disease which causes sickness and diarrhoea
evacuee	someone sent out of a city during bombing raids, for their safety
gunpowder	an explosive powder
latrine	a lavatory in an army camp or barracks
pissdale	a conveniently placed lavatory on a ship
press-gang	a system of forcing people to become sailors
revolution	a rebellion that overthrows the government
siege	surrounding a place in order to attack it or prevent people from leaving
trench	a deep ditch from which soldiers fought in the First World War

TIMELINE

Trojan Wars: c1200BC

Pre-historic ten-year war waged against Troy by the Greeks, ending in the burning of Troy.

Crusades: AD 1095-1300

Military expeditions by European Christians to recover the Holy Land from the Muslims. There were seven crusades between 1095 and 1300.

Hundred Years War: 1337-1453

France and England fought repeatedly over this period. At the Battle of Agincourt in 1415 the English won a victory over the French in northern France.

English Civil War: 1642-49

Fought between the Royalists, who supported King Charles I, and the Parliamentarians, who supported the rights of the English Parliament. The Parliamentarians won and Charles was executed.

American Revolution or War of Independence: 1775-83

Fought between Great Britain and its colonies in North America. The colonies won independence from Britain.

French Revolution: 1789

A revolt in France by the people against the monarchy and aristocracy, resulting in the execution of King Louis XVI and Queen Marie-Antoinette in 1793.

Napoleonic Wars: 1793-1815

A major series of wars that took its name from the great French general Napoleon Bonaparte. Famous wars and battles included the Peninsula Wars (1808-1814), the Battle of Trafalgar (1805), in which the British Admiral Nelson was killed, and the Battle of Waterloo (1815), in which the British-Prussian army defeated Napoleon.

American Civil War: 1861-65

Fought between the Northern States of America (the Unionists) and the Southern States (the Confederates). The south, outnumbered by the northern troops, eventually surrendered.

Crimean War: 1854-56

This took place in the Crimea, a peninsular in the Black Sea. Britain, France, Turkey and Sardinia-Piedmont defeated Russia. The Crimean War included the infamous Charge of the Light Brigade

Zulu Wars: 19th century

The Zulus, or Bantu peoples, of south-east Africa (modern Natal) were led in the early 19th century by their powerful leader Shaka. By 1850 the Zulus had defeated all neighbouring tribes. They were eventually defeated by the British in 1879.

First World War: 1914-18

Conflict between the Allies (France, Russia, Britain, Italy and the USA), and the Central Powers (Germany, Austria-Hungary and Turkey). After four years of bloody fighting the Allies emerged as the victors.

Second World War: 1939-45

The biggest war in human history, with over 50 million casualties. The Allies (Britain, the Soviet Union, and the USA) defeated the Axis nations (Germany, Italy and Japan).

INDEX

Africa *5, 8, 10*
America *19, 20*
American Civil War *19*
American War of
    Independence *20*
animals *4, 8-9, 12, 16, 17, 24, 28*
Aztecs *12, 24*

Battle of Agincourt *7*
Battle of Trafalgar *14-15*
Battle of Waterloo *24*
Battle of Zama *8*
bombs *11, 28, 29*

Celts *24*
children *5, 28-29*
China *10, 11*
Crimean War *22-23, 25*
crusades *5, 10, 18*

disease *7, 12-13, 17, 18*

English Civil War *16, 21*

First World War *11, 26-27*
food *16-17, 29*
France *7, 14, 20, 21, 22, 25*
French Revolution *21*

gas *11, 27, 29*
Germany *28-29*
Greece *9*
gunpowder *5, 10, 11*
guns *4, 10, 14, 15, 27*

Hannibal *8*

Incas *12-13*
Italy *8*

Japan *6, 11*

medicine *14, 24-25*
Mongols *16*

Napoleon *20, 24*
Napoleonic Wars *7*
Native Americans *4*
Nelson *14-15*

Peninsular War *24*
perfumes *20-21, 25*

Romans *6, 8, 16, 25, 30*
Russia *22-23*

Second World War *11, 17, 28-29*
Shaka *10*
ships *14-15, 17*
Spain *12-13, 14*

Turks *22*

uniforms *18-19*

weapons *4, 5, 6, 10-11, 12-13,*
                28-29